Feeling My Feelings

Written by Shilpi Mahajan

Illustrated by Monami Debnath

atmosphere press

Character Name: Able
Super Power: Self Awareness

Able was born in NYC. Her love for yoga and mindfulness
comes from her mother. Her self awareness skills
make her extremely emotionally intelligent and empathetic.

Character Name: Chad
Super Power: Resilience

Chad was born in Chicago. His grit comes from his father
who fought for equal rights for everyone.
He is resilient and uses meditation to strengthen his grit.

Character Name: Zara
Super Power: Courage

Zara is a Muslim Syrian refugee. She immigrated alone with her sister
and her courage comes from taking that leap of faith
to create a better life for herself and her sister. She loves sports.

Character Name: Fy
Super Power: Compassion

Fy loves Science and Art. He loves painting the galaxy.
He is extremely compassionate and strengthens
his practice with a regular loving kindness meditation.

Feeling My Feelings

Character Name: Rosa
Super Power: Empathy

Rosa was born to parents who didn't speak English. She was bullied in school and now uses her experience to create a safe space for her classmates. She loves animals.

Character Name: Lee
Super Power: Perseverance

Lee loves Music and Theatre. She works hard and is extremely persistent. She empowers everyone around her to work hard. She is kind hearted and helps people in need.

Character Name: Sid
Super Power: Gratitude

Sid is born to immigrant parents. He has an attitude of gratitude and teaches people how the little things matter more than the big ones. He leads with empathy and joy.

Knock, knock, knock,

I need to open the door

There is a feeling visiting me

And I want to know it more

I would like to listen.

I would like to sense

I would like to notice.

I would like to be your friend.

I want to feel you in my body.

I want to see you with my eyes.

I want to understand why you are here,
Before we say our goodbyes.

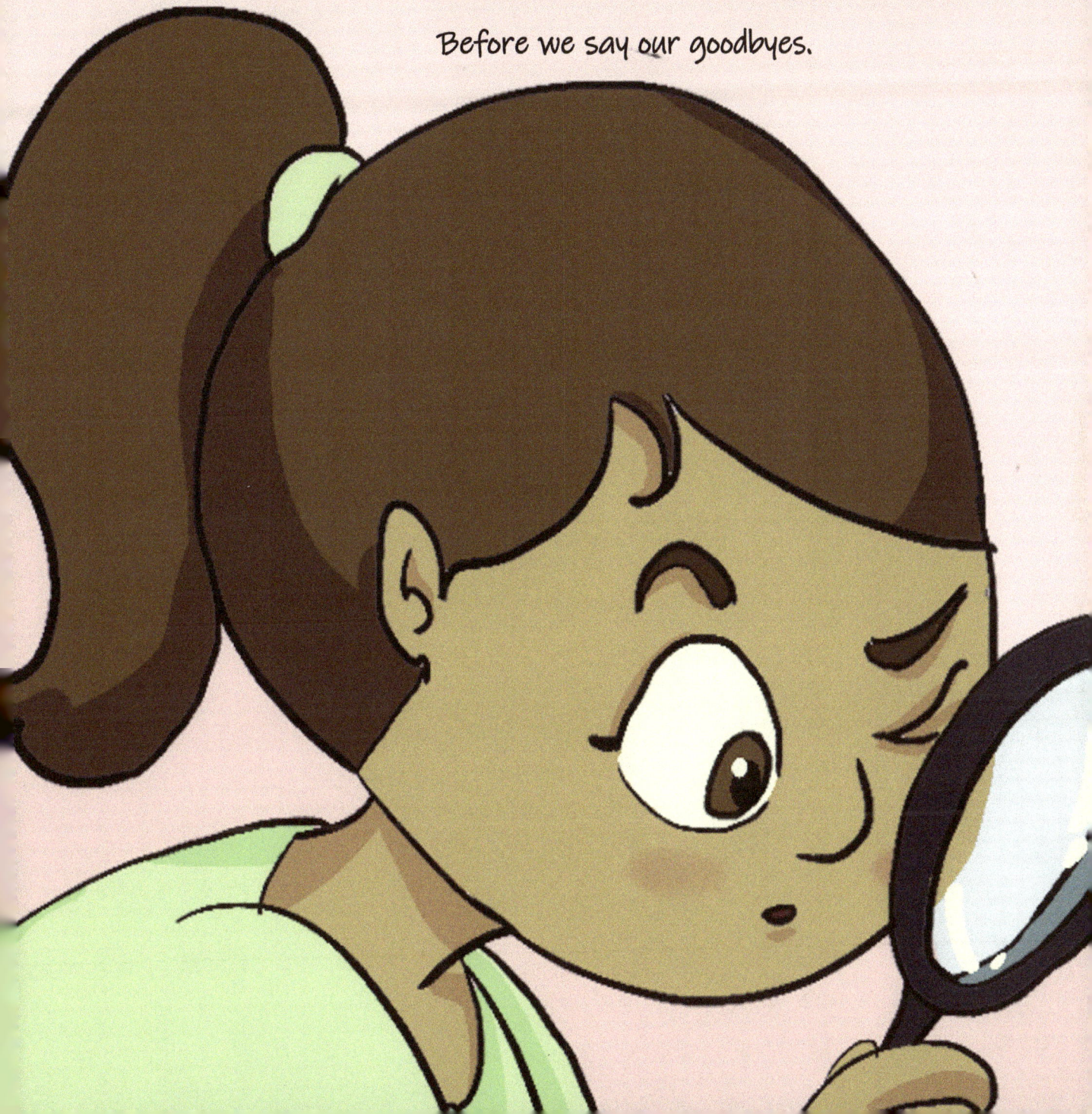

Are you warm like the sun,

Or are you cool like the moon?

Are you fluttery like a butterfly,

Or are you some looney tune?

Are you flowy like the river,

Or are you beautiful like a bird?

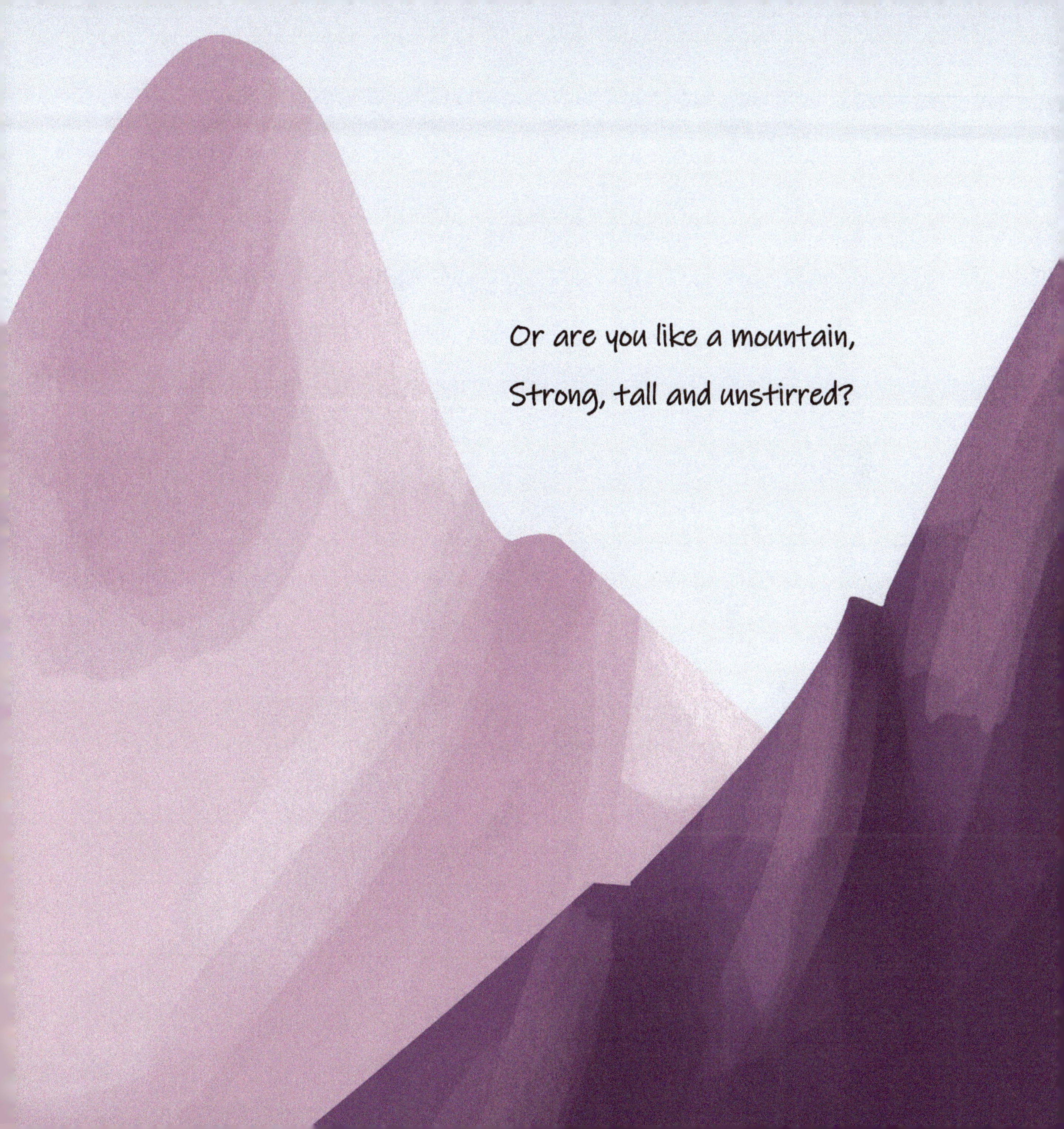

Or are you like a mountain,

Strong, tall and unstirred?

Are you soft like my teddy bear,

Or are you hard like a melon?

Are you sweet like honey,

Or are you sour like lemon?

Are you bitter like gourd,

Or are you salty like chips?

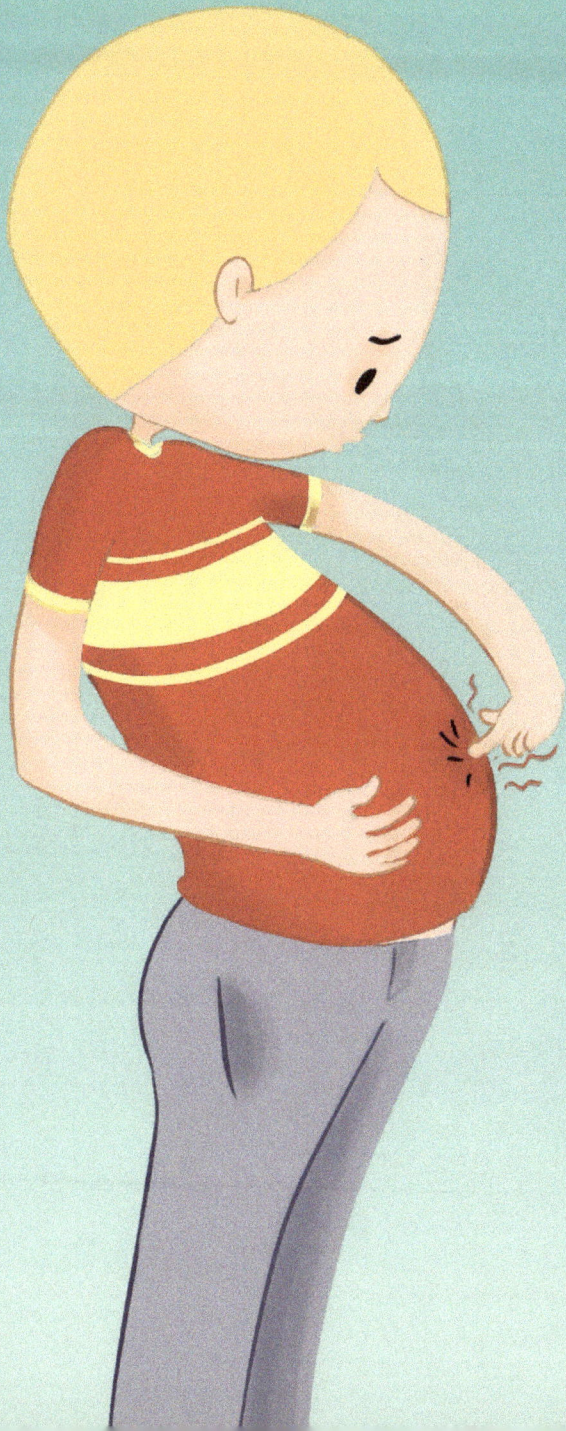

Are you hiding in my belly,

Or are you the movement of my lips?

Are you breathing fast in my chest,

Or are you the pain in my legs?

Are you the tingling in my shoulders,

Or are you humming in my head?

Hey, don't play hide and seek!

I need to know you better.

So that when you visit me again,

I will see you and remember.

My feeling is my friend,

And when I connect with you...

I can breathe softly,

Love myself and love you too.

The Mood Meter Exercise

The Mood Meter is a great Social Emotional Learning tool that helps children become aware of their emotions and over time helps them self-regulate them. It is based on Dan Siegel's concept of "Name it to Tame it". By naming and identifying an emotion, you learn to regulate the emotion.

Activity Name   Mood Meter

Activity Type   Individual Activity or Group activity

Duration   10-15 minutes

Objective(s) of the Activity   Creating a Mood Meter in your classroom helps children name their feelings. It is important to teach children to name the feelings because naming helps tame feelings. This activity can also be extended to home.

What's a Mood Meter?   The Mood Meter is a square or an arc divided into four quadrants – red, blue, green, and yellow – each representing a different set of feelings. Different feelings are grouped together on the Mood Meter based on their pleasantness and energy level.

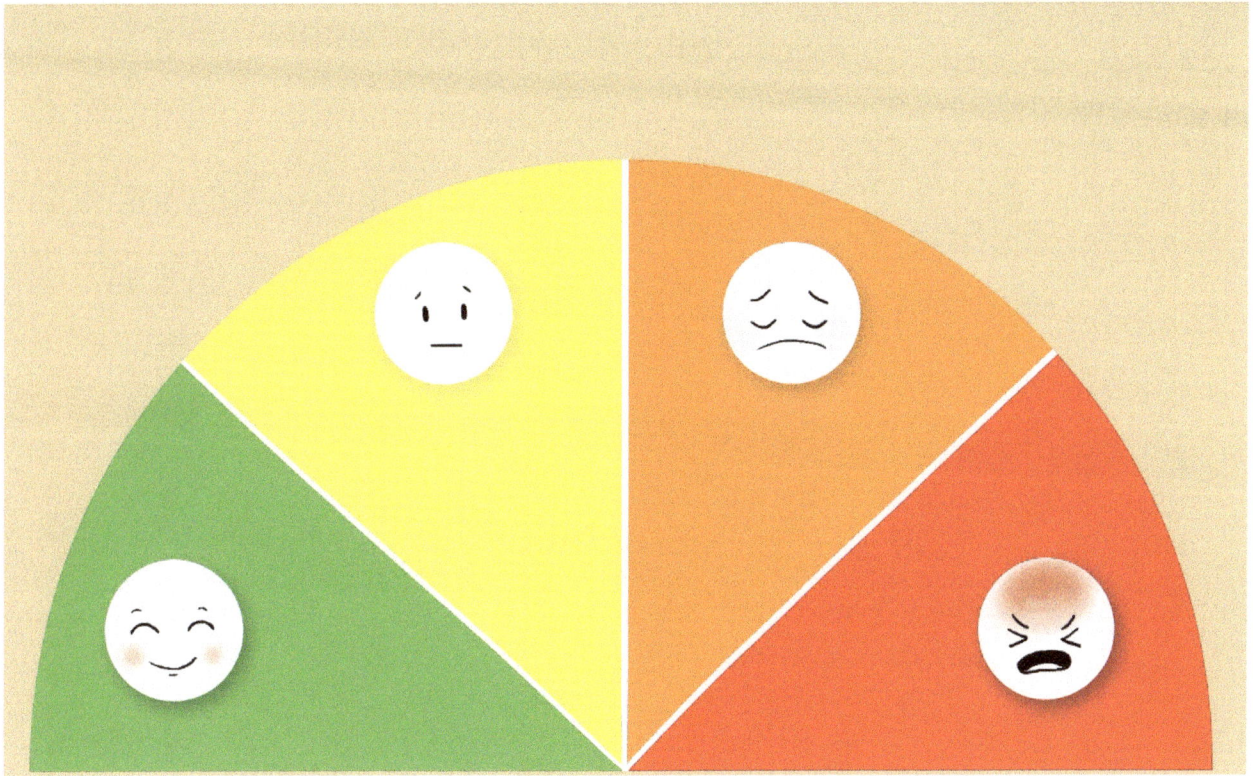

- RED feelings: high in energy and low in pleasantness (e.g., angry, scared, and anxious);
- BLUE feelings: low in energy and low in pleasantness (e.g., sad, disappointed, and lonely);
- GREEN feelings: low in energy and high in pleasantness (e.g., calm, tranquil, and relaxed);
- YELLOW feelings: high in energy and high in pleasantness (e.g., happy, excited, and curious).

Activity Details- How to Make a Mood Meter

Steps:

1. Ask your students to write a title on top of the poster board – such as, "Right Now, I Feel..."

2. Use your compass to make a large half-circle in the middle of your poster.

3. Use your ruler to divide the half-circle in half, and then divide each of the halves in half, so that you have four "slices" marked off.

4. Cut out a pie shape the same size as the "slices" on the half-circle using each color of construction paper—one green, one yellow, one orange, and one red.

5. Glue the colors from left to right across the half-circle in this order: green, yellow, orange, and red.

6. If the children are comfortable writing words, have them do the next step. If not, let them just read out the words. On the green slice, write "Calm and happy." For the yellow, have them write "A little upset." In the orange section, "Very upset." In the red, they can write, "Exploding!" or any word that indicates that they are extremely upset.

7. Together with your class, cut out a 6" long arrow from the black construction paper, and attach it to the poster board with the metal fastener. The arrow should be attached to the center of the flat side on the half-circle.

8. Let your students use markers and decorations to personalize the Mood Meter.

9. Put the "Mood Meter" in a prominent place in the classroom. (For home usage, a kitchen is a great area for placing the Mood Meter)

10. Invite your students to pay attention to how they are feeling and to talk about it.

Keep in Mind

This is an important emotional intelligence skill and you may want to create a separate corner for this in the class. You may want your students to create an extra one that they can carry home. Encourage them to use it with their parents.

To use the tool, encourage the class to plot their feelings several times throughout the day or week. You can use the colors of the
 to discuss their feelings. For example, you could say: "It seems you're in the red and you want to feel more green, is there something I can do to help?"

Once you've gotten used to identifying feelings with your class using the four colors, try attaching a specific word to the feeling.

For example, if someone is in the blue and feeling sad — ask them if there's another word that better describes how they feel. Are they lonely, disappointed, or melancholy? Say what you see, as you notice how the child expresses his or her feelings. "You're stomping your feet. You must be angry." Then, talk to the child about strategies for shifting awa y from this feeling. "If you're lonely, what can we do to help you feel less lonely and more connected?"

Encourage them to express their feelings. Let them say it without any judgement. Ask them for synonyms for their feelings so as to get more specific on how they feel.

Responses to Curb

Try not to mix feelings with thoughts.

Example: Thoughts are, "I didn't like when she snatched my pencil". However, examples of feelings are anger or sadness.

If a child says, "I didn't like it when they made fun of me." You can ask them to express the feelings through the Mood Meter. "I am feeling sad or dejected." Focus on the feeling and not the thoughts.

Don't try to get judgmental about feelings.

Example: Avoid saying things like "Don't be angry, anger is not good." Let them feel their anger so that over time, they learn to respond not react to that anger.

As students get used to the Mood Meter, they will know how to express themselves and it will help them resolve and self-regulate their emotions.

About Atmosphere Press

Atmosphere Press is an independent, full-service publisher for excellent books in all genres and for all audiences. Learn more about what we do at atmospherepress.com.

We encourage you to check out some of Atmosphere's latest releases, which are available at Amazon.com and via order from your local bookstore:

Beau Wants to Know, a picture book by Brian Sullivan

The King's Drapes, a picture book by Jocelyn Tambascio

You are the Moon, a picture book by Shana Rachel Diot

Onionhead, a picture book by Gary Ziskovsky

Odo and the Stranger, a picture book by Mark Johnson

Jack and the Lean Stalk, a picture book by Raven Howell

Brave Little Donkey, a picture book by Rachel L. Pieper

Buried Treasure: A Cool Kids Adventure, a picture book by Anne Krebbs

Young Yogi and the Mind Monsters, an illustrated retelling of Patanjali by Sonja Radvila

The Magpie and The Turtle, a picture book by Timothy Yeahquo

The Alligator Wrestler: A Girls Can Do Anything Book, children's fiction by Carmen Petro

My WILD First Day of School, a picture book by Dennis Mathew

The Sky Belongs to the Dreamers, a picture book by J.P. Hostetler

I Will Love You Forever and Always, a picture book by Sarah Thomas Mariano

Shooting Stars: A Girls Can Do Anything Book, children's fiction by Carmen Petro

Oscar the Loveable Seagull, a picture book by Mark Johnson

Carpenters and Catapults: A Girls Can Do Anything Book, children's fiction by Carmen Petro

Gone Fishing: A Girls Can Do Anything Book, children's fiction by Carmen Petro

Bello the Cello, a picture book by Dennis Mathew

That Scarlett Bacon, a picture book by Mark Johnson

Makani and the Tiki Mikis, a picture book by Kosta Gregory

About the Author

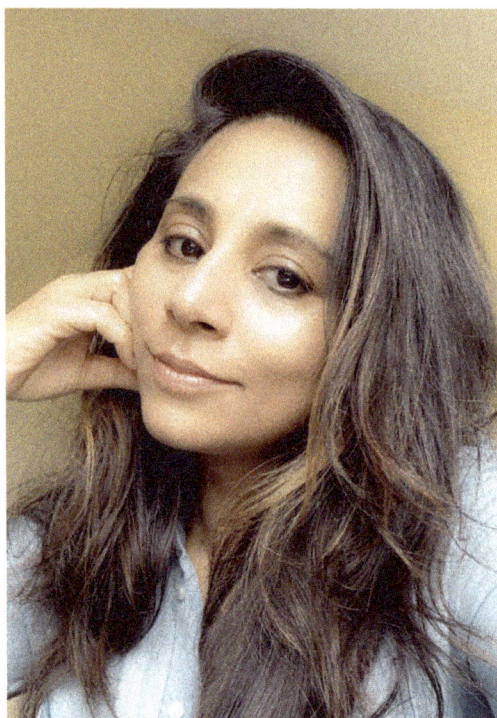

Shilpi has been practicing Mindfulness for seven years now. Trained in the Vipassana method of meditation, she introduced Mindfulness to her children about 5 years back and realized the importance of Mindfulness in bringing Social and Emotional Learning to kids, parents and educators. While meditation brought significant changes in her parenting, her stress and her relationships, what was pivotal were the life skills she was imparting to the kids. She chose to bring her learnings to children and parents and "Fablefy" was born. In the last one year, Fablefy has done significant work with "at-risk" kids, juveniles, and at the same time helping build strong communities through programs in the library. She has written three children's illustrated books on the subject.

In her previous avatar, Shilpi is an MBA (Finance) from Jamnalal Bajaj and worked in Finance and transformation roles in companies like Gillette, GE and IWMI.

CPSIA information can be obtained
at www.ICGtesting.com
Printed in the USA
LVHW071936310321
683089LV00017B/401